TRANSGENDER
RIGHTS AND ISSUES

BY ANDREA PELLESCHI

CONTENT CONSULTANT
Amy Stone
Associate Professor
Department of Sociology and Anthropology
Trinity University

Essential Library

An Imprint of Abdo Publishing | abdopublishing.com

abdopublishing.com

Published by Abdo Publishing, a division of ABDO, PO Box 398166, Minneapolis, Minnesota 55439. Copyright © 2016 by Abdo Consulting Group, Inc. International copyrights reserved in all countries. No part of this book may be reproduced in any form without written permission from the publisher. Essential Library™ is a trademark and logo of Abdo Publishing.

Printed in the United States of America, North Mankato, Minnesota
082015
012016

Cover Photo: Kevin Winter/Getty Images
Interior Photos: Jerry Holt/ZumaPress/Newscom, 4–5; R. Jeanette Martin/Demotix/ Corbis, 12; Witold Skrypczak/Alamy, 14–15; AP Images, 17; Dave Pickoff/AP Images, 25; Frank Franklin II/AP Images, 28–29; Bullit Marquez/AP Images, 30; Red Line Editorial, 37, 63; Olivier Douliery/ABACAUSA.COM/Newscom, 42; Jordan Strauss/ Invision/AP Images, 46–47; Peter Thoshinsky/ZumaPress/Newscom, 57; Steve Meddle/Rex Features/AP Images, 58–59; Mohammad Asad/Pacific Press/Sipa USA/ AP Images, 70; Pat Roque/AP Images, 72–73; Gerry Broome/AP Images, 75; Markus Scholz/EPA/Newscom, 80–81; Filippo Fiorini/Demotix/Corbis, 89; Todd Williamson/ Invision/AP Images, 90–91; XactpiX/Splash/Splash News/Corbis, 96

Editor: Mirella Miller
Series Designer: Maggie Villaume

Library of Congress Control Number: 2015944929

Cataloging-in-Publication Data

Pelleschi, Andrea.
  Transgender rights and issues / Andrea Pelleschi.
    p. cm. -- (Special reports)
  ISBN 978-1-62403-903-4 (lib. bdg.)
  Includes bibliographical references and index.
  1. Transgender people--Civil rights--Juvenile literature.   2. Transgender people-- Legal status, laws, etc.--Juvenile literature.   3. Transgenderism--Juvenile literature. 4. Transsexuals--Juvenile literature.   I. Title.
  306.76--dc23

2015944929

CONTENTS

CHAPTER ONE

A TRANSGENDER
HERO

CeCe McDonald may have been assigned male at birth in 1989, but she always knew she was meant to be a girl. Growing up as an African-American child in Chicago, Illinois, she enjoyed watching her mother and aunts try on different outfits and jewelry. At school, CeCe wore women's clothes, used the girls' bathroom, and became a cheerleader. "I wasn't born a boy," she said. "I was born a baby."[1]

The journey of becoming CeCe, which her friends called her because of her resemblance to the singer Ciara, was long and violent. It involved spending her teen years as a runaway and facing prison time as an adult. In the end, she became a hero for the transgender community.

Supporters gathered in Minneapolis, Minnesota, after CeCe McDonald was sentenced to prison.

MORE TO THE STORY

TRANSGENDER TERMINOLOGY

To talk about transgender issues, we need to understand the terms associated with them. The table below provides some common terms.

CISGENDER: Someone who is not transgender.

GAY: A person who is attracted to people of the same sex.

GENDER EXPRESSION: How a person shows his or her gender to the outside world through clothing, voice, or pronouns, such as "he," "she," or "they."

GENDER IDENTITY: How a person privately experiences his or her gender. If a man feels like a woman, his gender identity is female. If a man feels like a man, his gender identity is male.

LESBIAN: A woman who is attracted to other women.

LGBT: An acronym for lesbian, gay, bisexual, and transgender.

QUEER: Someone who feels outside the norms in terms of gender identity or sexual orientation.

SEX: Having male or female anatomy.

SEXUAL ORIENTATION: Determined by the gender(s) a person is physically or emotionally attracted to.

TRANSGENDER: A person whose gender identity differs from the gender he or she was assigned at birth.

SCHOOL LIFE

At school, CeCe did not try to hide her femininity. Because her family did not approve of her girlishness, she left the house in boys' clothes. She changed into her mother's blouse and platform shoes once she was at school. She used the girls' restroom instead of the boys' room. And she became a cheerleader at basketball games, doing splits on the gym floor just like all the other cheerleaders.

It was not easy being a transgender girl at school. The other students made fun of her, and some chased her through the neighborhood. CeCe liked to stand up for herself, which sometimes made the situation worse.

At home, CeCe tried to please her family by doing extra chores and preparing new recipes for the family. However, it did not help her family accept her as a girl. They asked CeCe to pray the girlishness out of her, and her mother encouraged her to be more traditional. After her uncle found a love note from CeCe to a boy at school, he knocked her to the kitchen floor and started choking her. That was when CeCe decided to run away.

RUNAWAY

At 14 years old, CeCe had no money and no place to live. At first she stayed with friends, but then she moved into a drug house with other runaways. For money, she sold crack and marijuana, and at 15 years old, she became a child prostitute. Despite the harsh conditions in which she lived, CeCe liked taking care of herself and making her own living. She felt empowered. She also was happy she could dress as a girl whenever she wanted to.

Over the years, though, the harsh lifestyle took its toll. CeCe was attacked several times for being transgender. She tried drugs, went in and out of shelters, and was arrested for shoplifting. She attempted suicide numerous times.

MINNEAPOLIS

When she was 18 years old, CeCe took a bus to Minneapolis, Minnesota. It was on a whim, a way to start over and change her life. By 2008, CeCe had earned her general equivalency diploma (GED), a test that provides students with the equivalent of a high school diploma. Then she went to college for fashion design. After that, CeCe saw a doctor about changing her body to match her gender identity. The doctor diagnosed her with gender dysphoria, a term that describes someone whose biological sex does not match his or her gender identity. The doctor prescribed female hormones for CeCe, which made her hips fuller and allowed her to grow breasts.

As CeCe's outer self began to match her inner self, her self-confidence grew. After years of not talking to her mother, CeCe reestablished ties with her. CeCe also legally changed her name to Chrishaun Reed Mai'luv McDonald. It was a name she chose because of how mystical it sounded and because her aunt was named Chrishaun, which gave CeCe a connection to the past. By May 2011, CeCe was able to move into her own apartment and leave homelessness behind.

Just one month later, though, CeCe had a confrontation that changed her life. After midnight, while walking to a 24-hour grocery store, she and her friends passed a bar. Some people who were standing outside the bar smoking started yelling insults at CeCe and her friends. CeCe talked back. "Excuse me," she said. "We are people, and you need to respect us."[3] No one listened to her. Instead, 40-year-old Molly Flaherty hit CeCe on the face with a drinking glass, which cut her cheek open. A fight broke out between CeCe's friends and the patrons of the bar.

CeCe walked away from the fight, but 47-year-old Dean Schmitz ran after her. He had drugs in his system and also had an arrest record for assault. When CeCe saw him running toward her, she reached into her purse and grabbed a pair of scissors she used in fashion school. As Schmitz lunged at CeCe, her scissors went into Schmitz's chest. CeCe ran away to get help as Schmitz fell to the ground and died soon after.

TRIAL AND PRISON

At the police station that night, CeCe confessed to everything, telling police she was defending herself. Other witnesses backed her up. They said Flaherty had smashed CeCe's face with a glass, and that Schmitz had run after CeCe. The problem was that no witnesses had seen exactly how Schmitz had been stabbed, so the prosecutors charged CeCe with second-degree murder. If convicted, she could go to prison for up to 40 years.

While awaiting trial, CeCe was locked up in jail. And to keep her from being hurt by other prisoners, she was kept alone in her own cell for 23 hours a day. It was a hard, lonely time. Luckily, CeCe was able to get a lawyer who could take her case pro bono, which meant the lawyer would not charge a fee.

The case drew the attention of the Minneapolis transgender community, and CeCe became a hero to others who had experienced similar

PRONOUNS

The pronoun *she* is used throughout CeCe's story because that is how she refers to herself. In general, it is best to ask transgender persons which pronoun they would prefer: *he*, *she*, or *they*. If it is not possible to ask, then go with the pronoun that matches the person's appearance and demeanor.

KYLE ANDREW SMITH SCANLON

TRANS RIGHTS ARE HUMAN RIGHTS!

CeCe's sentencing, along with the treatment of other transgender people, sparked protests across the globe for more equal rights for transgender people.

harassment. Activists circulated a petition and gathered 18,000 signatures for CeCe's release from jail. Supporters formed a Free CeCe organization and wore "Free CeCe" T-shirts during rallies outside the jail and then later during CeCe's trial.

At trial, prosecutors argued CeCe had stabbed an unarmed man without being provoked. In Minnesota, it is illegal to use deadly force against someone who is attacking you if you can run away. The prosecutors said CeCe should have run away. CeCe's lawyer thought the jury should know Schmitz was on drugs when he ran after her and that Schmitz had a prior record of assault.

Unfortunately, the judge would allow the jury to hear only a small part of this information. Because of this, CeCe pled guilty to second-degree murder. She received a prison term of 41 months.

After 19 months in prison, CeCe was released early for good behavior. Today, she is free and struggling to lead a normal life in Minneapolis. As an activist, she speaks before groups about her experiences as both a transgender woman and a former prisoner. In 2015, she gave a seminar at Rutgers University about humane prison systems. At Mills College the same year, she participated in a panel discussion about being a black transgender woman. In addition, a documentary is being made about her life that will examine the justice system and how it treats transgender women of color. "I *am* a survivor," CeCe says.[4] Yet she is so much more to the transgender community. To them she is a hero.

FREE CECE!

Laverne Cox, one of the stars of the television show *Orange Is the New Black* and a transgender woman herself, made a documentary focused on the attack that landed CeCe in prison. *FREE CeCe!* explores how transgender women dealt with violence and harassment similar to what CeCe experienced.

TRANSGENDER
HISTORY

Evidence of transgender men and women has been seen throughout history. Early explorers in North America saw signs of what we now call transgender people among the Native Americans. To the surprise of the Europeans, Native Americans were not judgmental about men and women who dressed, lived, and worked as if their gender was different from the one they were assigned at birth. Some tribes called these people "two-spirit," meaning they had the spirit of both a man and a woman. In contrast, European settlers often had strict religious views that called for men and women to act as their outward gender and marry the opposite gender. In the American colonies

In the 1530s, Spanish conquistador Álvar Núñez Cabeza de Vaca was the first to write about Coahuiltecan men dressing, living, and working as women. They also married other men.

during the 1600s and 1700s, people who dressed as the opposite gender were considered sinful.

By the late 1800s, cities in the United States grew to allow more diversity. Those who believed they were a different gender or expressed their gender in nontraditional ways were able to build their own communities. Drags, or masquerade balls, became popular in New York City among men who wished to dress in women's clothes and who wanted to socialize as women. While women at that time did not hold their own drags, they found other outlets to express their gender identity. Some went out in public dressed as men. Others performed as male impersonators in stage shows. In the 1920s, a blues singer named Gladys Bentley wore men's clothing both on and off the stage. Beginning in 1940, jazz musician Billy Tipton lived and performed as a man for almost 50 years.

MEDICAL ADVANCES IN SEX-REASSIGNMENT SURGERY

In the late 1800s and early 1900s, US and European doctors became interested in studying men and women who wore clothes of the opposite sex. A new field of medicine called sexology developed. The most influential doctor of this time was Richard von Krafft-Ebing, an Austro-German psychiatrist. He wrote a study in 1886 called *Psychopathia Sexualis* that described how strongly men or women felt about their own gender. According to Krafft-Ebing, on one end of the spectrum, cross-dressers might be interested in wearing the clothes of the opposite gender. On the other

No one knew Tipton, *center*, had been born a female until he died in 1989.

end of the spectrum, they might feel as if they were born with the wrong sex.

At Hirschfeld's Institute for Sexual Science, Dr. Felix Abraham performed the first sex reassignment surgery in 1922. The patient was Dorchen Richter, a man who believed he should be a woman. Richter had a second surgery to finish physically transitioning from a man to a woman in 1931. The clinic's most famous patient, however, was a Dutch painter who started life as Einar Wegener and became Lili Elbe in the 1920s.

During the 1930s, a significant breakthrough in the study of hormones occurred. Endocrinologists discovered men and women have both estrogen and testosterone. Estrogen is a female sex hormone. Testosterone is a male sex hormone. While both men and women have these hormones, women have much more estrogen in their bodies than men. And men have much more testosterone in their bodies than women. This means doctors can give estrogen to men who wish to transition to women. And they can give testosterone to women who wish to transition to men. From 1939 to 1949, Michael Dillon, a British doctor, used a combination of hormones and surgeries to transition from a woman to a man. He was the first person to do so.

In the 1950s and 1960s, one of the leading endocrinologists was Dr. Harry Benjamin. He believed hormone therapy and surgery were the best ways to treat individuals who believed they had been assigned the wrong gender at birth. According to Benjamin, psychotherapy was a waste of time. He called people who wanted to change their gender transsexuals.

LILI ELBE

Lili Elbe, a Danish artist, was one of the first people in the world to have sex reassignment surgery. Born in Denmark in 1882 and given the name Einar Mogens Wegener, she lived as a man for more than 20 years. The first time Wegener became "Lili" was when Wegener's wife, Gerda, an artist, needed a model for an illustration. Wegener donned stockings and high heels to become the dark-haired beauty who would pose in many modeling sessions. Soon Lili was dressing as a woman in public and going out with Gerda to parties. In 1930, Lili traveled to Berlin, Germany, to have sex reassignment surgery. One year later, she underwent an additional, risky operation. Unfortunately, this operation was not successful, and Lili died at the age of 48.

During this time, the medical community classified two different kinds of gender: biological sex and psychological sex. Another name for psychological sex is gender identity. Gender identity, doctors came to believe, was the main way people saw themselves. For example, an individual may have been assigned male at birth. But if his gender identity was female, then he was a female. Because of this, doctors said transsexual people should be able to change their gender to match their sense of self.

In the early 1950s, one of the most famous people to receive hormone therapy and sex reassignment surgeries was Christine Jorgensen. After she made the transition from a man to a woman, the newspapers picked up her story. She became a worldwide sensation. Suddenly, the concept of changing one's sex through surgery was something people could talk about. It raised awareness of transsexuals throughout the United States and the world.

In 1966, Johns Hopkins Hospital opened the first gender identity clinic, and within the first two and a half years, it received almost 2,000 requests for surgery. Ten years later, more than 40 gender identity clinics had been established throughout the United States.[1]

FIGHTING FOR RIGHTS

During the 1950s and 1960s, those whose gender did not conform to societal standards faced discrimination. It was hard for them to find work or an apartment to rent. If an ID card was required for a job, then it was hard for someone

MORE TO THE
STORY

CHRISTINE JORGENSEN

Christine Jorgensen is one of the most famous people to receive gender reassignment surgery. Born in 1926 as George Jorgensen, she grew frustrated as she got older and knew she wanted to be a woman. In the late 1940s, while still a clerk in the US Army, Jorgensen read an article about a Danish doctor who was experimenting with gene therapy. After flying to Denmark, Jorgensen received female hormone injections. The results were remarkable. Jorgensen's breasts grew larger. A bald patch on her head filled in with hair. And her body took on the contours of a woman.

In 1952, after more than one year of hormone therapy, Jorgensen underwent several operations that transformed her into a woman. She wrote to her family: "Nature made a mistake, which I have had corrected, and now I am your daughter."[2]

When Jorgensen flew back to New York, she was unrecognizable. Gone was the small, quiet army clerk. In his place stood a slim, glamorous woman in a fur coat. Tabloid newspapers loved her story and created headlines such as "Bronx GI Becomes a Woman." Hollywood embraced her, offering movie and theater contracts. During the 1960s and 1970s, she toured the country as a nightclub singer and impersonator. She died in 1989.

who identified as the opposite gender to obtain one that matched his or her appearance. Many people who lived and dressed differently from the rest of society had to live in cheap hotels and find work as prostitutes or maids. Many were arrested simply for being gay or for sending letters through the mail that were sexual in nature.

Two events helped launch the transgender rights movement in the United States. The first occurred in 1966 in San Francisco, California, at Gene Compton's Cafeteria. This 24-hour restaurant was popular with drag queens and gay men. Because the restaurant believed some of the patrons who were dressed as women were loitering, they called the police to remove them. When this occurred, protesters started a small riot and forced the police to back down. This is considered the start of the transgender rights movement.

The second event was in 1969, in New York City at the Stonewall Inn. At the time, there was a history of police raiding bars frequented by gays, lesbians, drag queens, and gender nonconformists. When the police raided the Stonewall Inn, a crowd gathered outside the bar. When the crowd saw what they believed was rough treatment of a patron, they began throwing things at the police. This led to six days of riots and is considered the start of the gay rights movement.

In 1970, two people involved in the Stonewall riots started the Street Transvestite Action Revolutionaries (STAR) in New York City. They were Sylvia Rivera and Marsha P. Johnson. By forming this group, they were able to help young people who were living on the streets and did not express their genders according to societal norms. In 1975, Minneapolis became the first city in the United States to offer legal protections for people with gender nonconformity. Also in 1977, the New York Supreme Court decided in favor of an athlete named Renée Richards. She was told she could play as a woman even though she was born a man.

The word *transgender* came into use in the 1980s. A California activist named Virginia Prince began using it to describe herself. To her, someone was transgender if they fell somewhere between a transvestite and a transsexual. This meant a transgender individual was someone who permanently changed his or her gender without the use of surgery. People became transgender by presenting themselves that way to the public. Then, in 1992, Leslie Feinberg wrote a pamphlet called *Transgender Liberation: A Movement Whose Time Has Come*. Her definition of transgender came to be a more general adjective: a "transgender man" or a "transgender woman." Feinberg called for all people who felt they did not fit societal norms of gender expression to band together to fight for their rights.

Despite these positive steps and rulings, the transgender rights movement continued facing resistance and discrimination. Activists spoke out against transgender individuals and said they had a disorder that could not be fixed through surgery. Because of this, and the fact that many in the medical community still did not believe in transgender surgery, clinics began closing, including the one at Johns Hopkins.

After this, more and more people spoke out for transgender rights. Public perceptions gradually began

The 1977 ruling said Richards could play professional tennis as a woman, despite being assigned male at birth.

changing. In 1986, an activist named Lou Sullivan formed the group Female-to-Male International, one of the first advocacy groups for transgender men. In 1993, Minnesota became the first state to offer legal support for transgender individuals and banned discrimination against them. In 1998, the first international Transgender Day of Remembrance took place to remember those who had lost their lives because of anti-transgender violence. And in 1999, the movie *Boys Don't Cry* was released. Based on the true story of the murder of a transgender young man, it brought awareness of the issue to millions of Americans.

In the 2000s and beyond, the transgender community continued gaining ground. San Francisco became the first US city to offer health coverage for transgender-related issues. It even provided money to transgender people who were city employees for sex reassignment surgery. In 2002, the Sylvia Rivera Law Project was founded to provide legal services to the transgender community. The following year, the National Center for Transgender Equality was formed to speak out for transgender equality and rights. In 2010, the federal government extended employment protection for transgender federal workers. And in 2012, the Equal

Employment Opportunity Commission (EEOC) declared employment discrimination against transgender people is a violation of the Civil Rights Act of 1964.

BOYS DON'T CRY

In 1994, 21-year-old Brandon Teena committed a small crime. When the newspaper reported on the crime, it disclosed that Teena had been assigned female at birth. Teena's friends, who knew Teena only as a guy, did not like this, so they assaulted and raped him. After Teena reported the incident to the police, the same friends then murdered Teena and two other people. This incident mobilized the transgender community to draw attention to the fact that transgender people often experience hate crimes. Newspaper articles, magazine articles, and books were written about the incident. In 1999, the movie *Boys Don't Cry* was made to tell Teena's story. Hilary Swank played Teena and won an Academy Award for her performance.

VIOLENCE AND
PREJUDICE

Despite gaining more rights over the years, the transgender community still experiences high incidences of violence from hate crimes and unfairness from the criminal justice system. Between 0.3 and 0.5 percent of Americans say they are transgender, which is approximately 1 million people in the United States.[1] The transgender community also faces discrimination in housing, employment, education, marriage, and many other areas of everyday life.

Some states and municipalities in the United States offer broad protections for transgender people, but many others offer few or no protections.

In recent years, the US government has passed legislation to support transgender rights. On the national level, this support addresses such areas as hate crimes, workplace discrimination, health care, and housing. On the state and local levels, legislation differs, depending on location. In addition, some employers offer their own protections for transgender individuals.

Jennifer Laude from the Philippines is one of many transgender women who are victims of hate crimes each year.

HATE CRIMES AND DOMESTIC VIOLENCE

The US Department of Justice defines hate crimes as "the violence of intolerance and bigotry, intended to hurt and intimidate someone because of their race, ethnicity, national origin, religion, sexual orientation, or disability."[2] Hate crimes against the LGBT community include physical violence, verbal harassment, discrimination, threats, intimidation, bullying, sexual violence, stalking, robbery, and other crimes. The most common hate crime is physical violence, which approximately 18 percent of LGBT people experience. Verbal harassment makes up 15 percent of LGBT hate crimes, and discrimination comes in third at 14 percent.[3]

In 2013, the National Coalition of Anti-Violence Programs conducted an extensive study of hate violence against lesbian, gay, bisexual, transgender, queer, and HIV-affected people. Transgender women were victims of more than 70 percent of the homicides against the LGBT community, including those with HIV. Almost all of these victims were women of color.[4] Yet transgender people

"JUST BEING TRANS[GENDER] OUT ON THE STREET IS CAUSE FOR OUR LIVES TO BE IN DANGER. SO MANY TIMES I'VE BEEN WALKING ON THE STREET AS A TRANS WOMAN AND BEEN HARASSED, CALLED A MAN—ONE TIME I WAS KICKED. ANY OF THEM COULD HAVE ESCALATED INTO SOMEONE DOING ME HARM."[7]

—LAVERNE COX, ACTRESS FROM
ORANGE IS THE NEW BLACK

make up only approximately 10 percent of the overall LGBT community.[5]

Members of the LGBT community do not always report problems to the police. In 2013, only 45 percent filed a police report about a crime that was done against them. This indicates many people in the LGBT community either face a barrier to reporting the crime or do not trust the police. More than half of the LGBT people who interacted with the police in 2013 felt their arrest was unjustified, and more than one-quarter felt the police used excessive force.[6]

There are two federal laws that help prevent violence against LGBT people. In 1994, Congress passed the Violence Against Women Act into law. This act requires individuals to help investigate and prosecute crimes against women, such as domestic violence, sexual assault, dating violence, and stalking. In 2013, the act was amended to include lesbian, gay, bisexual, and transgender women. The law has many provisions to reduce violence. For instance, it requires colleges and universities to provide students with information on domestic and dating violence. It also helps LGBT victims of domestic violence access shelters and other services.

In 2010, President Barack Obama passed the Matthew Shepard and James Byrd, Jr., Hate Crimes Prevention Act of 2009. This law makes it illegal to willfully cause injury to someone because of their race, color, religion, nationality, gender, sexual orientation, gender identity, or disability. It also ensures the federal government will help state and local governments prosecute hate crimes.

To help bring down the number of hate crimes, the National Coalition of Anti-Violence Programs recommends addressing the root causes of hate crimes. One of these root causes is poverty. When transgender people live in poverty, they are often forced to work in high-risk jobs such as prostitution and drug dealing. This places them in more dangerous environments and at a higher risk for violence. The coalition asks federal agencies to enforce rules that prohibit discrimination against transgender people in homeless shelters.

TRANSGENDER SURVIVOR STATISTICS (2013)

TRANSGENDER PEOPLE WHO SURVIVE VIOLENCE	COMPARED TO SURVIVORS OF ANY TYPE OF VIOLENCE
Transgender women	• 4 times more likely to experience police violence • 2 times more likely to face discrimination • 1.8 times more likely to be harassed
Transgender men	• 1.6 times more likely to experience police violence • 1.5 times more likely to be injured from hate violence • 4.3 times more likely to be the target of hate crimes in shelters
Transgender people of color	• 2.7 times more likely to experience police violence • 1.5 times more likely to face discrimination • 1.8 times more likely to be the target of hate crimes in shelters[8]

Another root cause of hate crimes is related to transgender people's reluctance to report crimes to the police. The coalition calls on municipalities to create policies and provide training that will help transgender people and the police interact in a more positive manner.

DISCRIMINATION IN PUBLIC PLACES

Transgender individuals experience discrimination in many areas of everyday life that the rest of society does not normally have to worry about. When it comes to shopping, eating in restaurants, going to the park or the library, seeing a movie, or visiting a bank, American transgender people can run into difficulties.

Seventeen states and Washington, DC, have laws making it illegal to discriminate against people because of their gender identity in public accommodations. However, 65 percent of transgender people say they have experienced discrimination in one of these public places, according to a 2014 study conducted in Massachusetts.[9] Bathrooms are particularly difficult places for transgender people to visit. They often suffer harassment and abuse when trying to use the appropriate bathroom.

FROM THE
HEADLINES

DISCRIMINATION LEADS TO POVERTY

In 2014, the Center for American Progress and the Movement Advancement Project released a report about the financial problems facing LGBT Americans. The report found LGBT people are much more likely to be poor than non-LGBT people. More than 20 percent of the LGBT community earns incomes less than $12,000 per year. This is compared to the 17 percent of the non-LGBT community. Transgender people fare even worse. Fifteen percent live in extreme poverty and earn less than $10,000 per year. Only 4 percent of the general population lives in extreme poverty.[10]

One thing that impacts poverty is the state or community in which an LGBT person lives. Some states have strict antidiscrimination laws for housing, education, credit, and marriage. Other states do not. LGBT poverty is always higher in states without antidiscrimination laws. One-third of LGBT people live in states without these protections. Even when states have antidiscrimination laws, the laws are often weak, and discrimination still exists. And discrimination can potentially lead a person down a path to poverty or keep them in poverty.

Extremely Low Income

Percent of transgender respondents reporting extreme poverty incomes less than $10,000 per year

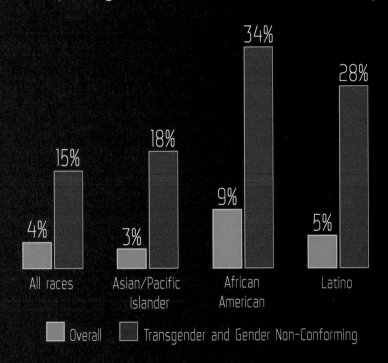

In schools, students often face bullying, harassment, and discrimination, starting from the time they are in elementary school through college. Up to 40 percent of gender-nonconforming young adults have experienced being harassed by other people at school, with a high number of that group experiencing verbal and physical abuse.[11]

Title IX of the Education Amendments of 1972 says that education programs and activities cannot discriminate based on which sex someone is. It applies to all public schools, as well as private schools, colleges, and universities that use federal money, and it is for students of all ages. Many people have questioned what Title IX means by discrimination based on sex. In 2014, the Office for Civil Rights (OCR) clarified exactly who is protected. The OCR

SCHOOL RESTROOM CASE

In 2007, when Nicole Maines was in fifth grade, she tried to use the girls' restroom. A classmate complained because Maines was a transgender girl. In response, the school told Maines she had to use the staff restroom. Maines's family sued the school district for discrimination. Seven years later, in 2014, Maines and her family won the lawsuit. The school district was not only ordered to let her use the restroom that matched her gender identity but also told it could not refuse this right to anyone else. Maines's case is the first time a state's highest court ruled a transgender person could use the restroom of his or her choice.

said Title IX applies to straight, gay, lesbian, bisexual, and transgender students. If someone is discriminated against because of gender identity or for not being masculine or feminine enough, they are protected under Title IX.

In addition to the federal protections in Title IX, some states have their own protections for transgender students. Thirteen states have antidiscrimination laws for students, and 18 states have laws that make bullying illegal. More than 12 states have laws that say transgender students can participate in all school activities, including sports teams.[12]

DISCRIMINATION IN EMPLOYMENT AND HOUSING

Many transgender people in the United States experience discrimination at work or when trying to find a job. Eighteen states have laws making employment discrimination illegal, but almost 80 percent of transgender individuals say they have been harassed or discriminated against at work in some way. Discrimination can also occur in the hiring process. Between 13 and 14 percent of transgender people say they were not hired because of discrimination. Some transgender people also risk losing their jobs if they come out as transgender.[13]

Currently, transgender individuals who want to serve in the US military must hide the fact that they are transgender. If a physical exam finds they have had sex reassignment surgery, they can be denied admission or be kicked out of the service. However, this ban against transgender soldiers may be easing, at least in the US Army. Instead of mid-level officers being able to dismiss someone from the army for being transgender, the decision must now come from an officer at a higher level.

In 1964, the US Congress passed the Civil Rights Act to protect Americans from discrimination. One provision of the act, Title VII, dealt with employment. This title said it was illegal for employers to discriminate against people because of their race, color, religion, sex, national origin, disability, or age. Businesses could no longer discriminate when hiring, firing, setting wages, testing, training, or promoting. To enforce the law, the EEOC was created.

Since the creation of Title VII, there have been many questions as to what the law means when it says a company cannot discriminate based on sex. In December

2012, the EEOC announced that Title VII applied to everyone, including lesbian, gay, bisexual, and transgender people. However, the EEOC is somewhat limited in how it can enforce this interpretation of sex discrimination. If an employer decides to discriminate against a transgender person, the EEOC can take that employer to court. But the courts do not have to agree with the EEOC, and they can rule against it in the case. Since the courts can rule against Title VII with regard to private employers, President Obama took action where he could: with federal employees. In 2014, he signed an executive order stating discrimination against LGBT employees is forbidden when they work for the federal government or for a company contracted by the government. Unfortunately, this executive order does not apply to private companies, state, or local governments.

JOB DISCRIMINATION CASE

When Mia Macy applied for a job at the Bureau of Alcohol, Tobacco, and Firearms (ATF), she did not know she would be making history. As a firearms expert, she was offered a job as a ballistics forensics technician. After the ATF discovered she had changed her gender identity from male to female, they said the position had been eliminated. In June 2011, Macy sued the ATF for discrimination. The following year, the EEOC used her case to declare that Title VII bans employers from discriminating against someone because of his or her gender identity. In 2013, Macy won her case.

Kristin Beck and Joanna Eyles, both transgender women, speak in 2014 about their transition after leaving the US military.

Many transgender people also face discrimination when looking for housing. According to the 2011 National Transgender Discrimination Survey, 19 percent of transgender people have not been able to buy a house or rent an apartment because of discrimination. Approximately 11 percent of transgender people have been evicted for the same reason. For this reason, many transgender people end up living on the streets or moving from one homeless shelter to another. If they go to a shelter, they are turned away almost one-third of the time.[14]

In 1968, the Fair Housing Act was passed. This act makes it illegal to discriminate against people when they are looking for housing. Race, color, religion, familial status, national origin, disability, and sex are all protected. Recently, the Department of Housing and Urban Development, which enforces the Fair Housing Act, said sexual orientation and gender identity are included in the definition of sex. If someone is denied an apartment because he or she is transgender, the Fair Housing Act may protect that person if it can be proven he or she was denied the apartment based on gender identity.

HEALTH CARE AND MARRIAGE

In 2010, the Affordable Care Act was passed into law. This law made it illegal for US insurance companies to deny coverage for anyone because of preexisting conditions or to discriminate against them because of their sex. A preexisting condition is a medical condition someone

"THE STORY OF AMERICA'S LESBIAN, GAY, BISEXUAL, AND TRANSGENDER (LGBT) COMMUNITY IS THE STORY OF OUR FATHERS AND SONS, OUR MOTHERS AND DAUGHTERS, AND OUR FRIENDS AND NEIGHBORS WHO CONTINUE THE TASK OF MAKING OUR COUNTRY A MORE PERFECT UNION. IT IS A STORY ABOUT THE STRUGGLE TO REALIZE THE GREAT AMERICAN PROMISE THAT ALL PEOPLE CAN LIVE WITH DIGNITY AND FAIRNESS UNDER THE LAW."[15]

—PRESIDENT BARACK OBAMA, PRESIDENTIAL PROCLAMATION: LESBIAN, GAY, BISEXUAL, AND TRANSGENDER PRIDE MONTH, 2011 has or had before applying for insurance. In 2012, the Department of Health and Human Services clarified that "sex discrimination" included gender identity, which allowed more transgender people to get insurance than ever before. However, many insurance plans do not cover sex reassignment surgeries, hormone therapy, or other medical needs related to being a transgender individual. Plus, transgender people often cannot get medical care for routine services that a non-transgender person can easily get. For instance, a transgender man might need to see a doctor about his female organs. Because of ID-related issues or inconsistent information on health records, he might not be able to get this care.

In 2015, the Supreme Court ruled same-sex marriage was legal in all 50 states. This solved many unique marriage challenges for transgender people. Before this ruling, transgender people could face difficulty after a spouse died. In the court case *Littleton v. Prange*, for instance, Christie Lee Littleton tried to file a wrongful death suit after her husband died. The case was in Texas, which did not allow same-sex marriage at the time. After the court saw Littleton's birth certificate, which said she had been born a male, it decided Littleton was still a male, despite presenting as a female. This meant the Littleton marriage had been a same-sex marriage, which was illegal in Texas. Since the marriage was illegal, according to the court, it did not exist. Littleton lost her case.

RIGHTS ORGANIZATIONS

There are many organizations available to help with discrimination and violence against the transgender community. GLAAD (which originally stood for Gay & Lesbian Alliance Against Defamation) is a great resource. This media organization provides information and resources for the LGBT community. Transgender people and allies can visit GLAAD's website to find more transgender resource links. LGBT families can find support through the national organization PFLAG (which originally stood for Parents and Friends of Lesbians and Gays). The National Center for Transgender Equality is a social justice organization focused on educating and advocating on national issues that are important to transgender people. The Transgender Law Center works to end discrimination through attitudes.

TRANSGENDER
YOUTH

Transgender youth often experience issues such as bullying in school, having trouble using the restroom of their choice, and playing sports for the gender that fits their gender expression. Some young people leave home and have to deal with life on the streets. Others become an inspiration to other transgender young people.

Transgender adolescents and teens often have to deal with bullying at school. Bullying is behavior toward another person that is unwanted and aggressive. There is a power imbalance in bullying in which the bully has all the power. And the behavior is repeated over and over again. Bullying can be verbal, such as anti-LGBT remarks. Or it could be physical, such as

Jazz Jennings has served as a positive role model for transgender youth around the world.

MORE TO THE
STORY

JAZZ JENNINGS, RISING STAR

In 2005, when Jazz Jennings was five years old, she put on a one-piece swimsuit and declared she was a girl. One year later, Barbara Walters interviewed her on ABC News as the youngest person to transition from a boy into a girl. Soon Jazz became famous, and news programs wanted to keep up with what was going on in her life.

Jazz used her fame to become a spokesperson for transgender issues. One way she does that is through social media. The 14-year-old's Twitter account has more than 5,000 followers. On YouTube, she has more than 60,000 subscribers, and an interview with Katie Couric garnered more than 540,000 views.[1]

In 2013, Jazz was honored at the GLAAD Awards. In 2014, she was named a Human Rights Campaign youth ambassador. That same year, *TIME* magazine listed her in their Top 25 Most Influential Teens of 2014. She also coauthored a children's book in 2014 about a transgender girl called *I Am Jazz*. Recently she was named the face of a digital campaign for the skin care company Clean & Clear. And in 2015, Jazz and her family will be starring in a reality show on TLC called *All That Jazz*.

hitting, punching, and other forms of violence. Because of bullying, students might feel unsafe at school or miss classes. Some of them avoid school activities or skip school entirely. Others may smoke, drink alcohol, or take drugs to manage stress.

According to the National School Climate Survey from the Gay, Lesbian & Straight Education Network, approximately 60 percent of LGBT students experienced anti-LGBT remarks from fellow students in 2013.[2] These remarks could be about how a student expresses his or her gender, meaning how masculine or feminine the student is. Often other students use the word *gay* in a negative way, such as "He's so gay." Sometimes school personnel make insulting remarks as well. Approximately one-third of transgender students were called insulting names such as "tranny" or "he/she."[3]

Insults become harassment when someone torments another person over and over again. In 2013, approximately three out of four LGBT students were verbally harassed at school for their sexual orientation, and more than half of them for their gender expression.[4] Often the harassment took the form of cyberbullying, which occurs on a cell phone or over the Internet.

Sometimes students are physically attacked at school for being gay, lesbian, bisexual, or transgender. These attacks range from shoving and pushing to punching, kicking, or hurting someone with a weapon of some sort.

In 2013, approximately one in five LGBT students were physically assaulted at school because of their gender, their sexual orientation, or how they expressed their gender. Approximately four in ten LGBT students did not feel safe at school because of their gender expression.[5]

Often students do not report bullying to school authorities. They might not believe the school will do anything about the bullying. They might worry reporting

CYBERBULLYING

In 2013, approximately half of LGBT students experienced some form of cyberbullying.[6] Cyberbullies use an electronic device, such as a phone, tablet, or computer. They post messages to chat rooms, social media sites such as Tumblr or Facebook, and other websites. They also send threatening or insulting text messages to cell phones. It is virtually impossible to escape cyberbullying. Websites operate all day long, every day of the year. If someone does experience cyberbullying, it is important to save evidence of what is going on and report it to the website or cell phone provider. Experts recommend a victim of cyberbullying should not respond to the hateful messages. For more information on cyberbullying and what to do about it, visit http://www.stopbullying.gov or the National Crime Prevention Council online.

the bullying will make things worse. Sometimes students do not want to be thought of as tattletales, or they are worried someone may reveal their sexual orientation or gender identity if they report abuse. Unfortunately, many students have become used to harassment and think it is part of normal student life. In 2013, only one-third of bullied LGBT students who told their school about bullying felt like doing so made a positive difference.[7] Students said sometimes the school did not do anything or administrators told them to ignore what was going on.

"IT'S A SCARY THING WHEN YOU FIRST COME OUT AND TELL PEOPLE YOU'RE TRANSGENDER, BUT EVERYONE HAS BEEN GREAT. MY FRIENDS AT SCHOOL HAVE HELPED ME TO LIVE AN AUTHENTIC LIFE, TO BE WHO I AM."[8]

—MAKA BROWN, FIRST TRANSGENDER GIRL TO BE ELECTED PROM QUEEN IN UTAH

What should schools do about bullying? A government website about bullying, http://www.stopbullying.gov, recommends schools set up clear policies on bullying of LGBT students. If sexual orientation or gender expression are not part of a current bullying policy, then they should be added. When schools have clear guidelines against LGBT bullying, students feel safer at school and are less

GAY-STRAIGHT ALLIANCES

Gay-Straight Alliances (GSAs) are middle school or high school clubs for LGBT and straight students. The purpose of the clubs is to support other students, socialize in a safe environment, and fight against LGBT discrimination and hate. In 2013, schools with GSAs had fewer incidents of discrimination, harassment, and bullying than schools without these groups. One example of a GSA is in a Lexington, Kentucky, high school. In 2015, the Lexington GSA hosted an alternative prom for only LGBT students. Students were still free to go to the regular school prom, but many of them felt more comfortable at the Pride Prom.

likely to experience harassment. The website also recommends training staff on preventing bullying, creating gay-straight alliances in schools, and openly discussing bullying.

DISCRIMINATION

LGBT students, and particularly transgender students, might experience discrimination at school. This can take the form of people referring to them with the wrong pronouns, people criticizing the clothing they wear, how affectionate school authorities will let them be with someone of the same sex, and whether school authorities will let them express themselves in a nontraditional way. In addition, classrooms might not allow LGBT topics to be discussed, and teachers may not let students write about these topics in their papers.

Using the restroom or locker room can be a source of extreme anxiety for transgender students. The 2013 National School Climate Survey from the Gay, Lesbian & Straight Education Network found more than two-thirds of transgender students avoided using the restroom and a little more than half avoided locker rooms.[9] When transgender boys were forced to use the girls' restroom or when transgender girls were forced to use the boys' restroom, they felt unsafe or uncomfortable. The same was true for using locker rooms.

SPORTS

Title IX says schools cannot discriminate against students because of gender identity. But athletic policies vary from state to state, with only 13 states and Washington, DC, having specific laws making discrimination illegal.[10] As of 2012, most schools were not in compliance with Title IX. The federal government can penalize a school for not

> "I'M NOT ALLOWED TO USE THE REGULAR BATHROOMS OR LOCKER ROOMS BECAUSE STUDENTS HAVE COMPLAINED THAT IT MAKES THEM FEEL 'UNCOMFORTABLE,' BUT IN THE LONG RUN, ISOLATING ME MAKES ME FEEL LIKE I DON'T HAVE THE SAME RIGHTS AS EVERYONE ELSE DOES."[11]
>
> —JONAS VALENTINE, 18-YEAR-OLD SENIOR WHO LOBBIED FOR MORE GENDER-NEUTRAL RESTROOMS AT SCHOOL

TRANSGENDER ISSUES AT SCHOOL

SCHOOL EXPERIENCE	NUMBER OF STUDENTS
Could not take a date of the same gender to a school dance	1 out of 10 LGBT students
Experienced physical assault	1.5 out of 10 transgender students
Could not wear clothes that matched their preferred gender	3 out of 10 transgender students
Heard negative remarks about transgender students	3 out of 10 students overall
Could not use their preferred name at school	4 out of 10 transgender students
Experienced verbal harassment	6 out of 10 transgender students
Had to use a restroom or locker room that matched the gender they were assigned at birth	6 out of 10 transgender students[12]

being in compliance, for example by removing federal funds, but no school has lost any significant money from being in noncompliance. The way people fight to achieve compliance with Title IX is by bringing a lawsuit against a school, and that does not happen very often.

When it comes to sports, most school systems are reluctant to allow transgender students to play, particularly transgender girls. Some critics believe boys will pretend to be transgender girls because they will have a competitive advantage on girls' teams. Even though this situation is unlikely, schools with an inclusive sports program should be on the lookout for this kind of fraud.

Other critics say transgender girls are bigger and stronger than their female teammates or opponents. They argue transgender athletes could hurt their teammates or provide an unfair advantage to a team. But girls and boys in sports come in a wide range of body types. Athletes are used to playing and competing with people who are bigger, smaller, taller, and shorter than they are. So girls' sports teams should be able to accommodate transgender athletes. There is also an assumption that all males will outperform all females in sports, which is not true. A transgender girl is not necessarily bigger, taller, or more skilled than her teammates on the girls' team.

HOMELESSNESS

In 2010, there were between 1.6 and 2.8 million homeless young people in the United States.[13] Of that number, approximately 40 percent are LGBT, according to a 2012 report.[14] Diamond, a 19-year-old transgender girl, has slept on park benches and in shelters since leaving home. She grew tired of arguing with her mother over issues such as her attraction to men or the fact she is transgender. Twenty-year-old Torreano David Stanley has slept in the subways in New York City. Stanley describes himself as gender fluid, but presents as female most of the time. When Stanley's gender identity caused friction with

KYE ALLUM

In 2010, Kye Allum became the first openly transgender athlete to play for an NCAA Division I sports team. At first he kept his gender identity secret from his teammates on his George Washington University women's basketball team. But hearing them refer to him as "she" and "her" made Allum feel sick, as if he wanted to tear his own skin off. He could not focus on basketball, so he came out as a transgender man. Though the fans sometimes stared, Allum found that the players and other teams were supportive. "Sports is about winning," Allum said. "It's about competing. It's about respect. And it's about how you play the game. It's not about the body you were born into."[15]

Young people often leave home because they do not feel accepted by family members for their sexual orientation or gender identity.

his sister, he left her house even when it meant a period of homelessness.

Often when youth find a homeless shelter, they are turned away and forced to find somewhere else to stay. Shelters say the biggest barrier they have to serving more LGBT individuals is lack of funding from local, state, and government agencies. Another barrier is lack of space in shelters.

CHAPTER FIVE

THE MEDICAL
COMPONENT

Transgender people face unique challenges in their health care. Some of these challenges involve transitioning from a man to a woman or vice versa. Others deal with the psychological toll being transgender can take on a person. The World Professional Association for Transgender Health (WPATH) issued a set of guidelines called Standards of Care for the Health of Transsexual, Transgender, and Gender-Nonconforming People. These guidelines provide information on the physical, psychological, and medical aspects of being transgender.

According to WPATH, people might express themselves in ways that are not standard for their gender. Society expects men and women to behave in

Livvy James was diagnosed with gender dysphoria at ten years old and was anxious to share her new identity at school after summer break.

certain ways, and when they do not, they are exhibiting gender nonconformity. For instance, a man might not act very masculine. Or a woman might not act very feminine. Because of pressure from society, gender nonconformity can make people depressed and anxious. Only some people who express their gender in nonstandard ways have gender dysphoria. Someone with gender dysphoria experiences extreme distress and anxiety about his or her own gender.

It is important to note that not all people with gender dysphoria have surgery or hormone treatments. How a person comes to terms with his or her own gender identity is highly individual. Some people may have only hormone treatments. Others might take hormones and have surgery. And others may not use either of these options.

BRAINPOWER

Men and women have different brains. Men's brains tend to be larger than women's brains because men typically have a larger body mass overall. The neurons and the chemical messengers in men's brains are slightly different, too. In the 1990s, scientists compared the brains of heterosexual men with those of transgender women. Both of these groups were designated male at birth, so their brains should be the same. The study, however, showed the brains of transgender women more closely matched those of women. These results are interesting, but because so many things can influence how a brain works, experts warn not to draw a definite conclusion from this study.

HORMONE TREATMENTS

The first step in seeking hormone treatment for gender dysphoria is seeing a health-care professional who is familiar with this condition. The health-care professional will write a letter of support stating the transgender individual has a diagnosis of gender dysphoria and is able to make sound decisions.

Hormone treatment for transgender women is a two-step process. To suppress testosterone, transgender women take androgen suppressants. In addition, they take estrogen. Some of the changes these hormones create are an increase in breast tissue, slowed growth of body hair, reduction of muscle mass, and softening of the skin.

Hormone treatment for transgender men involves taking testosterone. Once a transgender man begins treatment, he experiences the same effects an adolescent boy experiences when his body suddenly produces more testosterone in puberty, such as acne and oily skin. In addition, testosterone causes menstruation to stop, produces hair on the body and face, coarsens the skin, and increases lean muscle mass.

FROM THE HEADLINES

LEGAL DOCUMENTS

When people begin identifying as another gender, they may want to change their legal documents, such as their driver's license, passport, birth certificate, and social security card. The process can be long, expensive, and difficult. Also, the process differs depending on the state. To change one of these legal documents, someone might have to fill out several applications, pay filing fees, publish notices of name change in the newspaper, and perhaps get a background check. As of 2014, only 21 percent of transgender people have updated all of their legal documents with the correct gender.[1]

To change your gender on a passport, the US State Department does not require proof of gender reassignment surgery. It does, however, want to see proof of "appropriate clinical treatment for gender transition to the new gender."[2] Changing a driver's license depends on the state in which a person lives. Approximately half the states do not require someone to get gender reassignment surgery.[3] One way states are making this process simpler is by having the transgender person fill out part of a standard form and then having their physician fill out the other half.

It is much harder to change a birth certificate than other legal documents. This is because a birth certificate is considered a necessary official record by the government. Many state and local agencies require someone to obtain a court order, proof of gender reassignment surgery, or both.

STATE ISSUES NEW BIRTH CERTIFICATE AND DOES NOT REQUIRE SEX REASSIGNMENT SURGERY

STATE REQUIRES PROOF OF SEX REASSIGNMENT SURGERY TO AMEND OR ISSUE NEW BIRTH CERTIFICATE

STATE DOES NOT ISSUE NEW BIRTH CERTIFICATE OR AMEND EXISTING DOCUMENTS

This map shows what US states require in order to change a birth certificate in 2015.

Before some types of surgery are possible, such as removing male or female sex organs, a person must undergo 12 months of hormone treatments. Other kinds of surgery, such as breast removal, require the person to live as the opposite gender for 12 months.

SURGERY

When a transgender woman has surgery, it is called male-to-female surgery. Because hormone treatments do not enlarge the breasts enough, some transgender women have breast enlargement surgery. They also might have genital surgery. This surgery removes the testicles and changes the penis into a vagina.

In addition, some transgender women have plastic surgery to make their appearance more feminine. Because female brows are higher than male brows, forehead reconstruction is an option. Also, the nose, chin, and jaw can be reshaped to be more feminine. The Adam's apple can be shaved to be less prominent.

"WHAT PATIENTS REALLY EXPERIENCE IN TERMS OF THEIR EMOTION AFTER SURGERY IS A SENSE OF RELIEF MORE THAN ANYTHING. THEY FEEL LIKE THEY'RE ONE WITH THEIR SOUL, FINALLY."[4]

—DR. MARCI BOWERS, A DOCTOR WHO HAS HELPED MORE THAN 1,500 TRANSGENDER PATIENTS, 2015

When a transgender man has surgery, it is called female-to-male surgery. One procedure most transgender men have is to have their breasts removed and reshaped. This is to make the chest look more masculine. They also often have a hysterectomy, which removes their internal female organs, such as the uterus and ovaries. A less common procedure is to construct a penis. Unfortunately, the results are not satisfactory. Many surgeons in the United States have stopped performing this surgery.

CHAZ BONO

One of the most popular singing groups in the 1960s and 1970s was the duo of Sonny and Cher. They had their own television show, and they would sometimes bring out their daughter, Chastity, wearing frilly dresses and sporting curly blonde hair. Chastity was not typically feminine in real life. While she was young, she did not like wearing girls' clothes or having a pink bedroom. In 1995, she came out as a lesbian and later as a transgender man. After hormone treatments and breast removal surgery, Chastity became Chaz. To help raise awareness for transgender people, he appeared on *Dancing with the Stars*.

CHILDREN AND ADOLESCENTS

There is some controversy over how to treat transgender children and adolescents. Children as young as two years old may feel they are a different gender. However, a study from 2008 published in *Development Psychology* showed only 12 to 27 percent of transgender children still believe they are transgender when they become adults.[5] Often a child's feelings of gender dysphoria disappear before adolescence. For this reason, experts often suggest children take on a name and gender of the opposite sex for a period of time to see how they like it. This can be a period of exploration for the child, which may or may not lead to a permanent gender identity change.

For those children who still believe they are transgender when they reach puberty, this can be a time of anxiety. During puberty, young people become aware of their sex organs more than before. It can be stressful for them to see their own bodies change into a gender that does not fit their own sense of self. Body aversion can develop, which is when a person hates his or her own body.

Some adolescents begin taking hormones to delay puberty. The benefit of this treatment is that it gives young people more time to explore their gender. It also prevents them from developing male or female characteristics, which they may want to change in the future. This treatment can last for several years.

If an adolescent wants to continue medically transitioning into the opposite gender, then he or she could begin hormone treatments. These treatments are similar to those used for adults but modified for the changing characteristics of a young person's body. However, these treatments are not completely reversible. For instance, testosterone causes a person's voice to deepen. So if a young person decides not to medically transition from female to male and stops hormone treatment, her voice will stay deeper than it would otherwise be. However, the benefit of taking hormones at this time is that a young person will go through puberty as a person of the opposite sex.

HEALTH ISSUES

Transgender individuals face some health issues unique to

TRANSGENDER FIVE-YEAR-OLD

Even though he was assigned female at birth, Jacob Lemay knew he was a boy when he was just two years old. Mimi Lemay, Jacob's mother, noticed him poking at himself. "He was talking about hating his body," said Mimi. She heard him "saying things like 'Why did God make me this way?'"[6] Because Jacob was so unhappy, the Lemays made the difficult decision to let him change from Mia to Jacob. He was just four years old. Right now, at age five, Jacob is thrilled to be a boy. Someday he might receive hormone treatments and surgery to make his transition more permanent, but that decision can wait until puberty. In April 2015, the Lemays went on *The Today Show* to tell their story.

their population. For instance, transgender people suffer higher rates of violence, which can lead to injuries. They often lack health insurance and so may put off going to a doctor longer than other people. They experience a greater number of suicidal thoughts than the general population.

Perhaps the most alarming health issue for transgender people is the high suicide rate they have compared with the general population. In 2014, researchers from the American Foundation for Suicide Prevention and the Williams Institute at UCLA School of Law analyzed data from the National Transgender Discrimination Survey. The survey found 41 percent of all US transgender and gender-nonconforming people have attempted suicide. This is nine times the national average.[7] Researchers found discrimination and violence can lead to an even higher risk of suicide in transgender people. In addition, suicide attempts are higher for those who are homeless and those who have been turned away from a doctor because of being transgender. Researchers also found it did not matter how well educated transgender people were, how much money they made, or whether they were married or not. The suicide risk for transgender people and those who are gender nonconforming was still as high.

To help prevent suicide, a San Francisco group created the Trans Lifeline. This is a suicide prevention center where all of the workers are transgender. The hotline is a place where transgender people do not have to explain themselves before they can talk about their issues. In addition, the Trevor Project Lifeline is geared toward people 24 years and younger, and the Suicide Prevention Hotline is available 24 hours a day to help anyone who calls.

Another health issue some transgender people experience involves HIV. Once people become infected with HIV, they have it for life. Transgender women are most prone to this disease because they so often are involved in risky behaviors that lead to HIV infection, such as prostitution. Some studies show as many as 28 percent

of transgender women test positive for HIV. The number is greater for African-American women, at 56 percent, than for white women and Latinos.[9] Unfortunately, there is not much data on HIV infections in transgender men because there have been very few studies about this group. The Centers for Disease Control and Prevention is working to prevent further HIV spread by helping community-based organizations, funding researchers, and creating awareness campaigns.

The LGBT community and allies rally in Bangladesh to raise awareness for HIV.

CHAPTER SIX

THE
OTHER SIDE

Discrimination against transgender people and others in the LGBT community is common in the United States. LGBT people sometimes express ideas that are against some people's religion. Others feel that LGBT people do not need to be singled out for special protections. And yet others believe being transgender is a mental illness.

AGAINST RELIGION

Many Christian religions in the United States believe that being transgender goes against God's plan. The Bible says, "So God created man in his own image, in the image of God created he him; male and female created he them."[1] This means God created men and

An anti-LGBT protester calls attention to his sign during a parade.

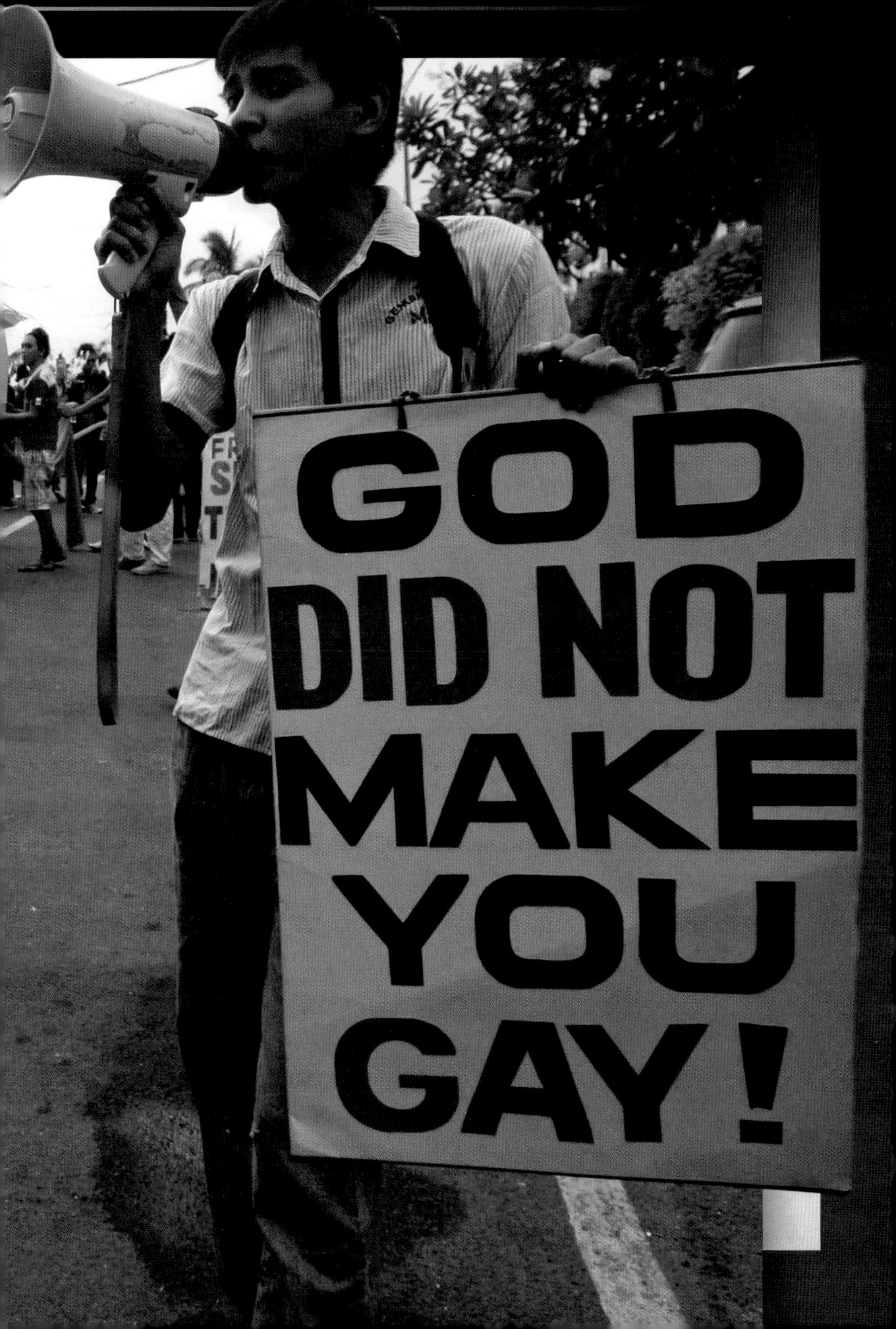
GOD DID NOT MAKE YOU GAY!

women as separate and unique people, and they should stay that way. Having surgery to change that, according to these groups, is unnatural and goes against God's plan for humans.

In 2014, the Southern Baptist Convention issued a resolution on transgender people. The resolution said a person's gender is a gift from God and should not be altered. According to the resolution, gender comes from biology and not from the way people feel about their own gender. To that end, the Southern Baptist Convention has vowed to fight any effort that makes being transgender acceptable to society as a whole. They also declared that, despite loving transgender people, they oppose any efforts by them to alter their bodies.

In addition, many conservative groups believe transgender people should not seek to change their gender. Focus on the Family is one such group. They describe themselves as a "global Christian ministry dedicated to helping families thrive."[3] Based on biblical principles, they provide resources to help marriages and families grow according to God's design. Their view of transgender people is that God made men and women as separate entities in his image. Those who believe they were born as the wrong gender are confused and "sexually broken."[4] Focus on the Family fights for laws and educational policies that keep the two genders separate.

The Alliance Defending Freedom is a legal organization founded in 1994 that fights for the rights of people to live freely in their faith. They believe their religious freedom is in danger from the growing acceptance of LGBT issues in society, including sexual orientation and gender identity. The Alliance Defending Freedom urges religious

The Southern Baptist Convention is one of the largest religions in the United States, with millions of followers.

organizations to create a statement of faith that clearly states their positions on sexuality and gender identity. This will help them avoid lawsuits or being legally forced to operate in ways that violate their religious beliefs.

Many religious and conservative groups, such as the Alliance Defending Freedom, feel it is a violation of their religious freedom to serve someone who is LGBT.

RELIGIOUS FREEDOM

The federal government has a law called the Religious Freedom Restoration Act of 1993 (RFRA) that protects religious groups from the actions of the federal government. Since 1993, 19 states have passed their own RFRA laws.[5] If a florist does not believe in gay marriage, for instance, he or she can refuse to sell flowers to a same-sex couple who is getting married. Some states with RFRA laws also have laws that ban discrimination against LGBT individuals. In those cases, the antidiscrimination laws might protect a same-sex couple who wishes to use the florist in the example. It becomes a case of balancing the religious rights of other people against the rights of LGBT people.

For instance, in 2011, a Macy's employee refused to allow a transgender woman to use the ladies' fitting room to try on a wedding dress. The employee cited religious reasons for her actions, and Macy's fired her because she violated store policy. In their defense, religious groups cite the First Amendment of the US Constitution, which states: "Congress shall make no law respecting an establishment of religion, or prohibiting the free exercise thereof."[6] The idea of refusing service to someone for religious reasons is controversial. It pits religious rights against the rights of LGBT people to use public accommodations.

MENTAL DISORDER

Dr. Paul R. McHugh was the psychiatrist-in-chief at Johns Hopkins Hospital from 1975 to 2001. In the 1970s, he was one of the people responsible for closing the Johns Hopkins clinic that treated transgender people with hormones and surgery. In 2014, Dr. McHugh published an editorial in which he stated that being transgender was a mental disorder. He said it was biologically impossible to change one's gender, and the desire to do so should not be treated with surgery. When surgery is used, it does not change a man into a woman. It changes a man into a feminized version of man, but he is still a man. The same is true of women.

Dr. McHugh has impressive credentials. As the author of six books and more than 120 articles, he is an expert in the field of behavioral sciences. However, most major medical organizations refute his opinions, including the

American Medical Association, the American Psychological Association, and the World Professional Association for Transgender Health.

CONVERSION THERAPY

Many Christian groups believe an LGBT person can be "repaired" to become more socially acceptable. They believe in a controversial system called conversion therapy. The idea behind the therapy is that a person's sexual orientation or identity can be changed through prayer and other religious means. Many critics say the therapy is dangerous and the idea of changing someone's sexual orientation or identity is wrong. In early 2015, the Obama administration spoke out against conversion therapy. "The overwhelming scientific evidence demonstrates that conversion therapy, especially when it is practiced on young people, is neither medically nor ethically appropriate and can cause substantial harm," said senior adviser Valerie Jarrett.[7] In May 2015, the Supreme Court decided to let a ban on conversion therapy stand. This sends the message that any state can ban conversion therapy without facing a challenge in court.

In addition, Dr. McHugh refers to a Swedish study from 2011 that says transsexuals have a higher rate of suicide after surgery. McHugh implies surgery makes their situation worse. The study in question reaches a different conclusion, though. They conclude that, even though suicide rates might be high, this means surgery is not enough to treat gender dysphoria. Further treatment is still needed.

SPECIAL PROTECTIONS NOT NEEDED

One argument against anti-LGBT discrimination laws

is that they are not needed. Ohio had a law banning same-sex marriage. In 2015, Ohio Attorney General Mike DeWine defended the law by saying the LGBT community has grown too powerful. LGBT people are not politically invisible, which means they are not powerless. Only minorities who are powerless deserve special protections.

Governor Bobby Jindal of Louisiana also believes LGBT people should not be protected as a special class. "My concern about creating special legal protections," he said, "is historically in our country, we have only done that in extraordinary circumstances. It doesn't appear to me we're in one of those moments today."[8]

TRANSGENDER PRIEST

Reverend Dr. Cameron Partridge transitioned from a woman to a man more than ten years ago. Today he is one of seven openly transgender clergy in the Episcopal Church. He is also the Episcopal Chaplain at Boston University and a lecturer at Harvard Divinity School. Partridge says he is proud to be part of a church that pushed for acceptance of all people. In 2014, he became the first openly transgender priest to preach at the National Cathedral in Washington, DC.

TRANSGENDER RIGHTS AROUND THE WORLD

The rights of LGBT people vary around the world. More than 1.3 billion LGBT people live in countries that grant them some protection. Unfortunately, a much higher number of people—2.7 billion—live in countries where they are at risk of being imprisoned or put to death for being gay. In fact, it is illegal to be gay in more than 70 countries around the world.[1] In Iran, Mauritania, Saudi Arabia, Sudan, and Yemen, the punishment for being gay is death.

In 2011, the United Nations (UN) General Assembly put together an annual report on human rights for

LGBT Pride participants in Germany hold a sign hoping a similar parade will be held in Iran in the future, if Iran changes its LGBT laws.

people around the world based on their sexual orientation and gender identity. The report found a pattern of violence and discrimination against LGBT people and recommended countries protect LGBT individuals from violence due to hate crimes. The UN's position is that no one should be arrested simply because of his or her gender identity or sexual orientation.

LATIN AMERICA AND NORTH AMERICA

In Latin America, most of the countries allow consenting LGBT adults to have sex with each other. Far fewer countries protect LGBT rights in other areas. Eleven countries have laws that make it illegal to discriminate against LGBT people at work, and only three countries have a law protecting the rights of LGBT people to marry: Saint Maarten, Argentina, and Uruguay. Four other countries give LGBT people some rights to marry, including Brazil, Ecuador, Colombia, and Costa Rica.[2] People are not very well protected against hate crimes in Latin America, and only some countries have anti–hate crime legislation.

All North American countries allow LGBT people to have consensual sex without legal barriers. Only Canada, however, has an antidiscrimination law in place for all LGBT workers. The United States has some laws that prohibit discrimination against LGBT people in the workplace, but other countries in this region do not have any laws, or their laws are not clear.

Canada and the United States allow same-sex marriage. Canada provides the most protection against LGBT hate crimes. The United States provides some protection, and the rest of the region does not provide clear protection.

EUROPE AND AFRICA

As a whole, Europe offers the most rights and protections for LGBT people. All 51 countries in this region allow consenting adults to have sex without legal barriers.

Nineteen countries provide full legal protection in the workplace, and another 22 countries provide some protection for LGBT workers. Ten countries make same-sex marriage legal. But 27 countries do not allow same-sex couples to marry, or their laws are unclear. Approximately half of the countries of Europe have hate crime laws that offer LGBT people at least limited protection from hate crimes. Unfortunately, this means 25 countries do not offer any protection, or their laws are unclear.[3]

African countries offer the fewest protections for LGBT individuals. In fact, most of the rights that are available in other regions are not available to most people in Africa. Consensual sex between LGBT adults is only legal in 22 out of 58 countries. In the rest, it is either illegal or the laws are unclear. Only eight countries have laws that make workplace discrimination illegal. Out of 58 countries, only South Africa has a law protecting the rights of LGBT people to marry. Two other countries give LGBT people some rights for marriage: Mayotte and Réunion, both of which are French colonies. Hate crime laws are missing throughout the entire continent except for Réunion.[4]

ASIA AND OCEANIA

In total there are 45 countries in Asia, and they offer some of the fewest rights in the world. Approximately half of the countries allow LGBT adults to participate in consensual sex. Only Israel has a law making anti-LGBT discrimination illegal in the workplace. The other 44 countries do not protect the rights of LGBT workers. As for LGBT marriage rights, Asia fares the worst in the world. None of the countries protect the rights of LGBT individuals to marry, and only two countries provide some protection: Israel and Palestine. Timore-Leste is the only country to have specific anti–hate crime legislation for LGBT individuals.[5]

Oceania includes Australia, Fiji, Guam, New Zealand, Samoa, and 18 other countries. Fourteen out of these

ZANELE MUHOLI

Zanele Muholi, an acclaimed South African photographer, makes her career capturing the images of LGBT people in beautiful black-and-white photographs. When she first started out as a journalist and photographer for an LGBT online magazine, Muholi was discouraged because she saw so few LGBT people represented in the media. "I wanted to fill a gap in South Africa's visual history that, even 10 years after the fall of apartheid, wholly excluded our very existence," she said.[6] Muholi's photographs have appeared in galleries throughout the world, and she has a website she shares with another photographer. It archives images of South African LGBT people and the stories that go along with them.

23 countries protect the rights of LGBT people to have consensual sex. This means another nine countries make consensual sex illegal or their laws are unclear. Only three of these countries protect LGBT workers' rights. And only New Zealand gives LGBT people the right to marry the person they choose. Australia gives LGBT individuals some marriage rights. The other 21 countries grant them no right to marry, or their laws are unclear. Only New Zealand offers specific hate crime protections for LGBT individuals. The rest of the region does not offer these protections, or their laws are unclear.[7]

IMPROVING CONDITIONS AROUND THE WORLD

To reduce hate crimes and eliminate LGBT discrimination, the UN has several recommendations. Countries should pass laws making hate crimes illegal. They should set up systems that make it easier for victims to report crimes and also for prosecutors to bring wrongdoers to justice. And finally, countries should allow LGBT people to seek asylum, or refuge, if they are being mistreated or tormented due to their sexual orientation or gender identity.

The UN also addresses laws that make it illegal to be LGBT in certain countries. The UN recommends countries repeal those laws. In addition, countries should create new laws that make discrimination against LGBT people illegal. Countries should provide education about LGBT issues so people will be less likely to discriminate against them.

INDIA'S THIRD GENDER

In 2014, the Indian Supreme Court recognized transgender people as a third gender. This means that transgender individuals will not have to choose "he" or "she" when they fill out government documents, such as ballot forms. They can choose "other." The government also granted transgender people the same help they give other minorities, including jobs and education. Called *hijras*, Indian transgender people often work as singers and dancers. They live at the margins of society and many have to beg or go into prostitution to survive. When the court awarded transgender people their rights, it said, "Recognition of [transgender people] as a third gender is not a social or medical issue but a human rights issue."[8]

FROM THE
HEADLINES

ARGENTINA

In 2012, Argentina enacted one of the world's most liberal laws for changing gender on official documents. In the past, before transgender people could change their gender, they had to get a diagnosis of gender dysphoria from a doctor and present their case in court. Now, under the new law, they do not have to do either of those things. All they have to do is want to change their gender. In addition, the law requires public and private doctors to provide hormones and gender reassignment surgery free of charge, even for those under the age of 18.

Before the new law, life in Argentina for transgender people was hard. They often dropped out of school, stayed away from hospitals, and had trouble finding jobs. The new law will not change conditions right away for people, but it will make it easier for them. "I couldn't use public services because the name on the documents, the name my parents gave me, wasn't me," said Marcela Romero, the president of ATTTA, an Argentinian transgender activist group. "A person who doesn't have an identity, doesn't have rights."[9]

In 2014, Denmark became the second country to pass a law similar to Argentina's. Around the world, other countries are showing signs of progress. Some European countries have dropped

Changing legal documents became much easier for transgender Argentines in 2012.

the surgical requirement from changing gender on legal documents, as have some states in the United States. Other countries, such as Pakistan, Germany, India, and New Zealand, offer the choice of a third gender on these documents.

A GROWING
ACCEPTANCE

Even though transgender individuals still face discrimination across the United States, the tide is turning. More and more transgender people are appearing in movies, on television, and in other forms of media. This exposure to mass audiences is giving Americans an idea of what it is like to be transgender. This can lead to understanding and acceptance.

A 2015 survey by the Human Rights Campaign (HRC) polled potential voters for the 2016 elections. The purpose of the poll was to see how many people knew someone who is transgender and what they thought of them. The results showed 22 percent of voters personally knew a transgender individual or worked with someone who was transgender.

Laverne Cox's character on *Orange is the New Black* brings more exposure to transgender individuals and leads to more acceptance.

Of that group, a little more than half felt positively toward the transgender person.[1]

This growing acceptance is about more than just good feelings. It results in real benefits for transgender workers. Annually, the HRC Foundation works with Fortune 500 companies through a Corporate Equality Index, a report that rates companies on their LGBT equality. In 2015, approximately two-thirds of Fortune 500 companies provided protection for employees based on gender identity. And another one-third of these companies provided health-care benefits that were transgender-inclusive.[2]

TELEVISION

In the past, if you wanted to find a transgender character on television, you had to look at side characters such as prostitutes and killers. From 2002 to 2012, GLAAD kept track of how transgender characters were portrayed on television. They found more than half were shown in a negative way.

Today the landscape is very different. Shows such as *Orange Is the New Black, Transparent,* and *Glee* have recently featured sympathetic transgender characters viewers can relate to. In fact, Laverne Cox from *Orange Is the New Black* is herself a transgender actress. On the MTV network, she has a documentary called *Laverne Cox Presents: The T Word,* which is about transgender youths. MTV also has a television show called *Faking It* that presents an "intersex" character, someone with both male and female chromosomes. On HBO, the documentary *Three Suits* is about a tailor who has transgender people as clients.

Many of these shows are not on major networks. They are on

LAVERNE COX

Laverne Cox was born in Alabama as one of two twin brothers. Throughout school, Cox knew she was not a boy; however, she did not identify as a girl either. This led to bullying. As a defense and to prepare for the future, Cox worked to achieve straight As. In college she studied dance and acting. Her big break came when she was discovered on the subway dressed up in a vintage coat, box braids, and tons of makeup. A woman came up to Cox and declared that she would be perfect in her movie. Cox auditioned for the role and acted in the movie. After that, she decided to fully transition to a woman. In 2008, she appeared on a reality show on cable network VH1 as the first African-American transgender woman to do so. In 2013, she began playing the role of a transgender woman on the critically acclaimed show *Orange Is the New Black.*

smaller cable networks or online sites. Since non-network outlets such as Netflix do not have to first sell their shows to advertisers, they can be more daring with their story lines. Often the story lines use some anti-transgender language. And the transgender character may be the victim or the villain and not the hero of the story. But these shows illustrate the progress transgender people are making in popular culture. In addition, some of the shows are garnering major recognition for quality. *Transparent* won two Golden Globe awards in 2014, and Laverne Cox became the first transgender actor to be nominated for an Emmy.

OTHER MEDIA

Transgender characters have not been as common in movies as they have been on television shows. In its study of the entertainment industry, GLAAD found only one movie in 2013 that featured a transgender character, *The Dallas Buyers Club*. The film was critically acclaimed, and Jared Leto won an Oscar for his role. People in the transgender community were not happy that a transgender actor did not play his role, however,

MORE TO THE
STORY

CAITLYN JENNER

When Caitlyn Jenner, formerly known as Bruce, won the gold medal in the decathlon at the 1976 Summer Olympics, no one knew about her inner struggle of wanting to be a woman. At eight or nine years old, Jenner liked to try on dresses from her mother's and sister's closets when they were out of the house. Later on, while Jenner was on the road giving motivational speeches, she liked to go to her hotel room and dress in women's clothing. "[People] see you as this macho male," said Jenner during a 2015 interview with Diane Sawyer, "but my heart and my soul and everything that I do in life—it is part of me. That female side is part of me. That's who I am."[4]

In 2015, Jenner came out to the world as a transgender female. During her interview with Sawyer, she said she had undergone facial surgery to make her features more feminine. She also started receiving hormone treatments. Currently, Jenner and her family are on a reality show, *I Am Cait*, about their family. Jenner hopes the exposure from her show will help bring greater awareness to transgender issues worldwide. In 2015, Jenner accepted the Arthur Ashe Courage Award at the ESPYS, an award show sponsored by ESPN to recognize athletic achievements.

and this sparked a debate about using non-transgender actors for transgender characters. In 2014, none of the 114 movies released featured transgender characters.[5] In 2015, the movie *The Danish Girl* was released, which tells the true story of Lili Elbe, one of the world's first transgender women.

Jenner steps out in New York City in one of her first public appearances after her transition.

In the music industry, the punk band Against Me! helped bring awareness of transgender people to many Americans. The lead singer in Against Me! is a transgender woman who publicly transitioned, starting in 2012, from Tommy Gabel to Laura Jane Grace. And in 2014, Against Me! released an album that features Grace's transition. Titled *Transgender Dysphoria Blues*, the album features punk rock songs such as "True Trans Soul Rebel."

FASHION INDUSTRY

In the fashion industry, the line between men's and women's clothing is blurring. So is the line between male and female models. Supermodel Andreja Pejic is a transgender model who started out as both a men's and a women's model. Now she has completely transitioned to being a woman and is the face of Make Up For Ever. This makes her one of the first transgender models to be on a significant advertising campaign.

Recently, celebrities have started wearing clothing typical of the opposite gender. In late 2014, several fashion designers dressed their male models in women's clothing, including Gucci and Chanel. Several women's fashion

"NOBODY CARES ANYMORE. THE DISTINCTION BETWEEN MAN AND WOMAN IS DISAPPEARING, AESTHETICALLY AT LEAST. . . . AS A DESIGNER, YOU REFLECT THE CULTURE, AND THIS IS A BIG FACET OF OUR CULTURE RIGHT NOW."[7]

— LAZARO HERNANDEZ, COFOUNDER OF PROENZA SCHOULER, A NEW YORK–BASED DESIGNER OF WOMEN'S CLOTHING

designers, such as Givenchy and Giorgio Armani, did the same thing, dressing female models in men's clothing. In the spring of 2014, the store Barneys New York presented 17 transgender models in their spring 2014 campaign.[6]

TRANSGENDER RIGHTS GOING FORWARD

In the United States, transgender individuals still face many civil rights hurdles going forward into the 2010s. Discrimination in housing, employment, education, and access to public accommodations continues to be a problem. Many transgender people face bullying, harassment, and violence from hate crimes, as well as unfairness from the criminal justice system. While the federal government has clarified existing laws to include protections for people based on their gender identity, many states continue to discriminate against LGBT individuals.

Going forward, greater protections are still needed for transgender people, particularly at the state and local level. Activists should push state legislatures to add additional rights, such as making it easier for transgender people to change their identity on legal documents; obtain insurance coverage for medical transition procedures; and work and live where they would like.

In 2014, *TIME* magazine said transgender rights constituted the new civil rights frontier in the United States. Going forward, advocates must continue to speak out for these rights both in the United States and throughout the world so transgender people will enjoy the same rights as non-transgender people.

ESSENTIAL
FACTS

MAJOR EVENTS

- In 1922, at Hirschfeld's Institute for Sexual Science, Dr. Felix Abraham performs the first sex reassignment surgery when he reassigns the gender of a patient from a man to a woman.

- During the 1930s, a significant breakthrough allows men and women to use hormone treatment to help them transition to the opposite gender.

- In 2010, President Obama signs the Matthew Shepard and James Byrd, Jr., Hate Crimes Prevention Act of 2009, making it illegal to injure someone because of race, color, sexual orientation, gender identity, and other criteria.

KEY PLAYERS

- Dr. Felix Abraham performs the first sex reassignment surgery.

- Activist Leslie Feinberg brings the word *transgender* into popular use in 1992.

IMPACT ON SOCIETY

When Christine Jorgensen appeared on the front pages of newspapers in the 1950s, not many Americans knew about transgender people or their issues. Since then, a civil rights movement has raised awareness of the discrimination and violence transgender people face in their daily lives. Many federal, state, and local laws have been passed or clarified to protect transgender individuals, but there are still many areas in the country where discrimination is legal. However, transgender people are becoming more and more common in popular culture, such as in the show *Orange Is the New Black*. Familiarity with transgender people can lead to a growing acceptance among Americans, which can then lead to real benefits for the transgender community.

QUOTE

"The story of America's Lesbian, Gay, Bisexual, and Transgender (LGBT) community is the story of our fathers and sons, our mothers and daughters, and our friends and neighbors who continue the task of making our country a more perfect Union. It is a story about the struggle to realize the great American promise that all people can live with dignity and fairness under the law."

—*President Barack Obama, Presidential Proclamation: Lesbian, Gay, Bisexual, and Transgender Pride Month, 2011*

GLOSSARY

CROSS-DRESS
To wear the clothing made for the opposite sex.

DRAG QUEEN
A gay man who wears women's clothing, especially to entertain people.

ENDOCRINOLOGIST
A doctor who diagnoses and treats hormone imbalances and problems in the body.

GENDER NONCONFORMITY
When a person does not show their gender in line with societal norms for that gender.

HATE CRIME
An act of violence against a person because of their race, ethnicity, national origin, religion, sexual orientation, or disability.

HORMONE

A chemical in the body that regulates the function of specific organs or tissues in the body.

SEX

The classification of someone as male or female.

SEX DISCRIMINATION

To treat someone unfairly because they are male or female; this also includes treating someone unfairly for their sexual orientation or gender identity.

SEXOLOGY

The study of human sexual life or relationships.

SEXUAL ORIENTATION

A person's physical, romantic, and/or emotional attraction to another person.

TRANSGENDER

A person whose gender identity does not match the gender he or she was assigned.

TRANSITION

To change one's birth sex to that of the opposite sex.

TRANSSEXUAL

An older medical term that refers to a person who wants to change, or has changed, his or her body into the opposite sex.

ADDITIONAL
RESOURCES

SELECTED BIBLIOGRAPHY

"Standards of Care for the Health of Transsexuals, Transgender, and Gender-Nonconforming People." *World Professional Association for Transgender Health*. WPATH, 2015. Web. 8 June 2015.

Teich, Nicholas M. *Transgender 101: A Simple Guide to a Complex Issue*. New York: Columbia UP, 2012. Kindle.

"Understanding Issues Facing Transgender Americans." *GLAAD*. GLAAD, Feb. 2015. Web. 8 June 2015.

FURTHER READINGS

Andrews, Arin. *Some Assembly Required: The Not-So-Secret Life of a Transgender Teen*. New York: Simon, 2014. Print.

Hill, Katie Rain. *Rethinking Normal: A Memoir in Transition*. New York, Simon, 2014. Print.

WEBSITES

To learn more about Special Reports, visit
booklinks.abdopublishing.com. These links are routinely
monitored and updated to provide the most current
information available.

FOR MORE INFORMATION

For more information on this subject, contact or visit the
following organizations:

Human Rights Campaign
1640 Rhode Island Ave. NW
Washington, DC 20036
800-777-4723
http://www.hrc.org
This is a civil rights organization working for equality for lesbian, gay,
bisexual, and transgender Americans.

National Center for Transgender Equality
1325 Massachusetts Ave. NW, Suite 700
Washington, DC 20005
202-903-0112
http://transequality.org
Transgender activists who are trying to change policies to advance
transgender equality founded this organization.

SOURCE
NOTES

CHAPTER 1. A TRANSGENDER HERO

1. Sabrina Rubin Erdely. "The Transgender Crucible." *Rolling Stone*. Rolling Stone, 30 July 2014. Web. 26 June 2015.

2. Ibid.

3. Ibid.

4. Ibid.

CHAPTER 2. TRANSGENDER HISTORY

1. Laura Erickson-Schroth, ed. *Trans Bodies, Trans Selves: A Resource for the Transgender Community*. New York: Oxford UP, 2014. Print. 511.

2. Chloe Hadjimatheou. "Christine Jorgensen: 60 Years of Sex Change Ops." *BBC News*. BBC, 30 Nov. 2012. Web. 26 June 2015.

3. Laura Erickson-Schroth, ed. *Trans Bodies, Trans Selves: A Resource for the Transgender Community*. New York: Oxford UP, 2014. Print.511.

CHAPTER 3. VIOLENCE AND PREJUDICE

1. "GLAAD Media Reference Guide." *GLAAD*. GLAAD, 2015. Web. 26 June 2015.

2. "Hate Crime." *National Crime Prevention Council*. National Crime Prevention Council, 2015. Web. 26 June 2015.

3. Osman Ahmed and Chai Jindasurat. "Lesbian, Gay, Bisexual, Transgender, Queer, and HIV-Affected Hate Violence in 2013." *National Coalition of Anti-Violence Programs*. New York City Gay and Lesbian Anti-Violence Project, 2014. Web. 26 June 2015.

4. Ibid.

5. Sabrina Rubin Erdely. "The Transgender Crucible." *Rolling Stone*. Rolling Stone, 30 July 2014. Web. 26 June 2015.

6. Osman Ahmed and Chai Jindasurat. "Lesbian, Gay, Bisexual, Transgender, Queer, and HIV-Affected Hate Violence in 2013." *National Coalition of Anti-Violence Programs*. New York City Gay and Lesbian Anti-Violence Project, 2014. Web. 26 June 2015.

7. Sabrina Rubin Erdely. "The Transgender Crucible." *Rolling Stone*. Rolling Stone, 30 July 2014. Web. 26 June 2015.

8. Osman Ahmed and Chai Jindasurat. "Lesbian, Gay, Bisexual, Transgender, Queer, and HIV-Affected Hate Violence in 2013." *National Coalition of Anti-Violence Programs*. New York City Gay and Lesbian Anti-Violence Project, 2014. Web. 26 June 2015.

9. "Understanding Issues Facing Transgender Americans." *GLAAD*. GLAAD, Feb. 2015. Web. 8 June 2015.

10. "Paying an Unfair Price: The Financial Penalty for Being LGBT in America." *Center for American Progress* and *Movement Advancement Project*. Movement Advancement Project, 24 Nov. 2014. Web. 26 June 2015.

11. "Understanding Issues Facing Transgender Americans." *GLAAD*. GLAAD, Feb. 2015. Web. 8 June 2015.

12. Ibid.

13. Ibid.

14. Ibid.

15. "Presidential Proclamation—Lesbian, Gay, Bisexual, and Transgender Pride Month." *White House*. White House, 31 May 2011. Web. 26 June 2015.

CHAPTER 4. TRANSGENDER YOUTH

1. Emanuella Grinberg. "Why Transgender Teen Jazz Jennings is Everywhere." *CNN*. Cable News Network, 19 Mar. 2015. Web. 26 June 2015.

2. Joseph G. Kosciw, Emily A. Greytak, Neal A. Palmer, and Madelyn J. Boesen. "The 2013 National School Climate Survey." *GLSEN*. Gay, Lesbian & Straight Education Network, 2014. Web. 26 June 2015.

3. "GLAAD Media Reference Guide." *GLAAD*. GLAAD, 2015. Web. 26 June 2015.

4. Joseph G. Kosciw, Emily A. Greytak, Neal A. Palmer, and Madelyn J. Boesen. "The 2013 National School Climate Survey." *GLSEN*. Gay, Lesbian & Straight Education Network, 2014. Web. 26 June 2015.

5. Ibid.

6. Ibid.

7. Ibid.

8. Mitch Kellaway. "Utah High School Elects State's First Transgender Prom Queen." *Advocate.com*. Here Media, 2 May 2015. Web. 26 June 2015.

9. Joseph G. Kosciw, Emily A. Greytak, Neal A. Palmer, and Madelyn J. Boesen. "The 2013 National School Climate Survey." *GLSEN*. Gay, Lesbian & Straight Education Network, 2014. Web. 26 June 2015.

10. Pat Griffin. "Developing Policies for Transgender Students on High School Teams." *National Federation of State High School Associations*. NFHS, 21 Nov. 2014. Web. 26 June 2015.

11. Dan Moran. "Transgender Student Petitions for More Gender-Neutral Accommodations." *Chicago Tribune*. Chicago Tribune, 1 May 2015. Web. 26 June 2015.

12. Joseph G. Kosciw, Emily A. Greytak, Neal A. Palmer, and Madelyn J. Boesen. "The 2013 National School Climate Survey." *GLSEN*. Gay, Lesbian & Straight Education Network, 2014. Web. 26 June 2015.

13. "Gay and Transgender Youth Homelessness by the Numbers." *Center for American Progress*. Center for American Progress, 21 June 2010. Web. 26 June 2015.

14. Miranda Leitsinger. "Left Behind: LGBT Homeless Youth Struggle to Survive on the Streets." NBC News. NBCNews.com, 3 Aug. 2014. Web. 26 June 2015.

15. Katy Steinmetz. "Meet The First Openly Transgender NCAA Division I Athlete." *Time*. Time.com, 28 Oct. 2014. Web. 26 June 2015.

CHAPTER 5. THE MEDICAL COMPONENT

1. "Understanding Issues Facing Transgender Americans." *GLAAD*. GLAAD, Feb. 2015. Web. 8 June 2015.

2. "FAQ About Identity Documents." *Lambda Legal*. Lambda Legal, n.d. Web. 26 June 2015.

3. "Understanding Issues Facing Transgender Americans." *GLAAD*. GLAAD, Feb. 2015. Web. 8 June 2015.

4. "Inside the Practice of a Doctor Who Has Performed 1,500 Gender Reassignment Surgeries." *Huff Post OWN Videos*. HuffingtonPost.com, 1 Apr. 2015. Web. 26 June 2015.

SOURCE NOTES
CONTINUED

5. "Standards of Care for the Health of Transsexuals, Transgender, and Gender-Nonconforming People." *World Professional Association for Transgender Health*. WPATH, 2015. Web. 8 June 2015.

6. Jonathan Capehart. "Bruce Jenner, Jacob Lemay and What it Means to Be Transgender." *Washington Post*. WashingtonPost.com, 22 Apr. 2015. Web. 26 June 2015.

7. Emily Alpert Reyes. "Transgender Study Looks at 'Exceptionally High' Suicide-Attempt Rate." *Los Angeles Times*. Los Angeles Times, 28 Jan. 2014. Web. 26 June 2015.

8. Jonathan Capehart. "Bruce Jenner, Jacob Lemay and What it Means to Be Transgender." *Washington Post*. WashingtonPost.com, 22 Apr. 2015. Web. 26 June 2015.

9. "About HIV/AIDS." *Centers for Disease Control and Prevention*. CDC, 16 Jan. 2015. Web. 26 June 2015.

CHAPTER 6. THE OTHER SIDE

1. Jori Lewis. "Transgender and Christian: Finding Identity." *USC Annenberg*. Religion Dispatches, 2 Sept. 2009. Web. 26 June 2015.

2. Ashley Fantz. "An Ohio Transgender Teen's Suicide, A Mother's Anguish." *CNN*. Cable News Network, 4 Jan. 2015. Web. 26 June 2015.

3. Jeff Johnston. "Transgenderism: Blurring the Lines." *Focus on the Family*. Focus on the Family, 2012. Web. 26 June 2015.

4. Ibid.

5. Scott Bomboy. "Explaining the Indiana RFRA Controversy in Five Minutes." *National Constitution Center*. National Constitution Center, 1 Apr. 2015. Web. 26 June 2015.

6. Luke Brinker. "GOP Lawmaker: Gay People 'Don't Have a Right to be Served in Every Single Store.'" *Salon*. Associated Press, 5 Mar. 2015. Web. 26 June 2015.

7. Lawrence Hurley. "US Supreme Court Upholds Ban on Gay Conversion Therapy." *Christian Science Monitor*. Christian Science Monitor, 4 May 2015. Web. 26 June 2015.

8. Evan McMurry. "Jindal: Be Careful About Creating 'Special Rights' for Gays and Lesbians." *Mediaite*. Mediaite, 5 Apr. 2015. Web. 26 June 2015.

CHAPTER 7. TRANSGENDER RIGHTS AROUND THE WORLD

1. Feilding Cage, Tara Herman, and Nathan Good. "Lesbian, Gay, Bisexual and Transgender Rights Around the World." *Guardian*. Guardian News, n.d. Web. 26 June 2015.

2. Ibid.

3. Ibid.

4. Ibid.

5. Ibid.

6. Cristina Ruiz. "Photography: Zanele Muholi Shoots Down Prejudice." *ft.com*. Financial Times, 8 May 2015. Web. 26 June 2015.

7. Feilding Cage, Tara Herman, and Nathan Good. "Lesbian, Gay, Bisexual and Transgender Rights Around the World." *Guardian*. Guardian News, n.d. Web. 26 June 2015.

8. "India Court Recognises Transgender People as Third Gender." *CNN*. Cables News Network, 15 Apr. 2014. Web. 26 June 2015.

9. Emily Schmall. "Transgender Advocates Hail Law Easing Rules in Argentina." *New York Times*. New York Times Company, 24 May 2012. Web. 26 June 2015.

CHAPTER 8. A GROWING ACCEPTANCE

1. Liz Halloran. "Survey Shows Striking Increase in Americans Who Know and Support Transgender People." *Human Rights Campaign*. Human Rights Campaign, 24 Apr. 2015. Web. 26 June 2015.

2. Ibid.

3. Ibid.

4. Sean Dooley, Margaret Dawson, Lana Zak, Christina Ng, Lauren Effron, and Meghan Keneally. "Bruce Jenner: 'I'm a Woman.'" *ABC News*. ABCNews.com, 24 Apr. 2015. Web. 26 June 2015.

5. Whitney Friedlander. "GLAAD Report: Movies Improving for Gay Characters, Still Lack Transgender Roles." *Variety*. Variety Media, 15 Apr. 2015. Web. 26 June 2015.

6. Alice Gregory. "Has the Fashion Industry Reached a Transgender Turning Point?" *Vogue*. Vogue.com, 21 Apr. 2015. Web. 26 June 2015.

7. Ibid.

INDEX

ABOUT THE
AUTHOR

Andrea Pelleschi has been writing and editing children's books for more than 12 years, including novels, storybooks, novelty books, graphic novels, and educational nonfiction books. She has a master's of fine arts in creative writing from Emerson College and has taught writing classes for college freshmen. She currently lives in Cincinnati, Ohio.